Copyright © 2023 by P. C. Dictionaire (Author)

This book is protected by copyright law and is intended solely for personal use. Reproduction, distribution, or any other form of use requires the written permission of the author. The information presented in this book is for educational and entertainment purposes only, and while every effort has been made to ensure its accuracy and completeness, no guarantees are made. The author is not providing legal, financial, medical, or professional advice, and readers should consult with a licensed professional before implementing any of the techniques discussed in this book. The content in this book has been sourced from various reliable sources, but readers should exercise their own judgment when using this information. The author is not responsible for any losses, direct or indirect, that may occur from the use of this book, including but not limited to errors, omissions, or inaccuracies.

We hope this book has been informative and helpful on your journey to understanding and celebrating older adults. Thank you for your interest and support!

Title: A Language Unfolded-How History, Culture, and Language Converged
Subtitle: Discovering the Origins, Transformations, and Triumphs of English

Series: The Grammar Bible: Mastering the Rules and Conventions of English

By P. C. Dictionaire

"The English language is the sea which receives tributaries from every region under heaven."
Henry David Thoreau

"The English language is like a broad river on whose bank a few graceful trees are reflected, it is the language of a people who have a great past and who will have a great future."
Joseph Conrad

"The English language is the key to the world."
Neil Gaiman

"The English language is nobody's special property. It is the property of the imagination: it is the property of the language itself."
Derek Walcott

"The English language is the most important language in the world. It's the language of international business, politics, and entertainment."
Richard Branson

"The English language is a river that moves, and sometimes it flows backwards."
Alice Oswald

"The English language is a work in progress. Have fun with it."
Jonathan Culver

Table of Contents

Introduction
The importance and significance of language in human history and culture

Language is one of the defining features of human civilization. It allows us to communicate with each other, to express our thoughts and emotions, and to convey knowledge from one generation to the next. But language is much more than a tool for communication. It is a fundamental part of human culture and identity, shaping the way we see ourselves and the world around us.

In this book, we will explore the fascinating history of the English language, tracing its evolution from its earliest roots to the modern day. Along the way, we will discuss the many cultural and historical influences that have shaped the language into what it is today. But before we delve into the specific details of the English language, it is important to understand the broader significance of language in human history and culture.

Language is not just a means of communication. It is a fundamental part of our identity and culture, shaping the way we see ourselves and the world around us. From the earliest times, humans have used language to share knowledge, express emotions, and build social bonds. The ability to communicate effectively was essential for survival, allowing early humans to work together to hunt, gather food, and defend themselves against predators.

As human societies grew more complex, so did their languages. New words and expressions were developed to describe new ideas and technologies, and languages evolved to reflect the changing needs of their speakers. Language also became a way to express cultural identity and values. Different regions and groups developed their own dialects and languages, each with its own unique history and cultural significance.

Throughout history, language has played a crucial role in shaping human societies and cultures. It has been used to spread ideas and beliefs, to record history and literature, and to build bridges between different communities. The spread of languages through colonization, trade, and migration has led to cultural exchange and the blending of different traditions and practices.

Today, the English language is one of the most widely spoken and influential languages in the world. Its history and evolution reflect the broader story of human civilization, and studying it can provide valuable insights into the ways in which language, culture, and history are interconnected.

In the following chapters, we will explore the rich and complex history of the English language, from its earliest roots to its current global dominance. We will see how the language has evolved over time and how it has been shaped by historical events, cultural influences, and the ingenuity of its speakers. By understanding the history of the English language, we can gain a deeper appreciation for the role that language has played in human history and culture, and for the ways in which language continues to shape our world today.

The English language is one of the most widely spoken and influential languages in the world. It is the official language of over 50 countries and is spoken by more than 1.5 billion people worldwide. But how did this language become so ubiquitous, and what makes it so significant on a global scale?

In this book, we will explore the fascinating history of the English language, tracing its evolution from its earliest roots to the modern day. Along the way, we will discuss the many cultural and historical influences that have shaped the language into what it is today. But before we delve into the specific details of the English language, it is important to understand the broader significance of the language and its global reach.

English is not just a language. It is a global phenomenon that has come to dominate the worlds of business, science, and culture. From Hollywood movies to international trade agreements, English is the language of global communication. But why has English become so dominant, and what sets it apart from other languages?

One of the key factors behind the global spread of English is the history of British colonization. As the British

Empire expanded throughout the world, English became the language of administration and trade, and it was imposed on the colonized populations. This led to the development of English-based pidgin and creole languages in many parts of the world, which eventually evolved into distinct English dialects.

In the 20th century, the influence of the United States as a superpower further solidified English's position as the dominant global language. The rise of American culture and media has helped to spread English to all corners of the world, and it has become the default language of international business, science, and diplomacy.

But what sets English apart from other languages is its adaptability and flexibility. English has borrowed words from countless other languages, and it continues to evolve and change to meet the needs of its speakers. This has made English a truly global language, one that is constantly evolving and adapting to new cultural and linguistic contexts.

Today, the English language plays a crucial role in the global economy and in the exchange of ideas and information between different cultures. By studying the history and evolution of English, we can gain a deeper understanding of the ways in which language shapes our world and our interactions with each other.

In the following chapters, we will explore the rich and complex history of the English language, from its earliest roots to its current global dominance. We will see how the language has evolved over time and how it has been shaped by historical events, cultural influences, and the ingenuity of its speakers. By understanding the significance of the English language on a global scale, we can gain a deeper appreciation for its importance in the modern world.

The purpose and scope of the book

In this section, we will discuss the purpose and scope of this book, "A Language Unfolded - How History, Culture, and Language Converged".

The English language has a rich and fascinating history, and this book aims to provide readers with a comprehensive overview of its origins, transformations, and triumphs. Our goal is to explore the various influences that have shaped the language we know today, from its earliest origins to its global significance in the modern world.

The purpose of this book is to provide readers with a deeper understanding of the English language and its role in human history and culture. Whether you are a language enthusiast, a student of linguistics, or simply someone who enjoys learning about the world around you, this book will offer valuable insights and information.

Throughout the following chapters, we will delve into the evolution of the English language, exploring its roots in Old English and the various influences that have shaped it over time. We will examine the impact of historical events, such as the Norman Conquest, the Renaissance, and the Industrial Revolution, as well as the contributions of other languages, such as Latin, French, and German.

We will also discuss the global significance of the English language, from its role as a lingua franca in international business and diplomacy, to its use as a tool of cultural exchange and creative expression. By exploring the many facets of the English language, we hope to provide readers with a deeper appreciation of its complexity, beauty, and enduring importance in the world today.

Overall, the scope of this book is to offer a comprehensive overview of the English language, from its earliest origins to its global significance in the modern world. We hope that readers will find this book informative, engaging, and thought-provoking, and that it will inspire a deeper appreciation of the role that language plays in shaping our world.

This book, "A Language Unfolded: How History, Culture, and Language Converged", provides an in-depth look at the evolution of the English language, from its origins to the present day. The book is divided into six chapters, each covering a specific period of English history and its linguistic developments.

Chapter 1: The Origins of English This chapter delves into the prehistory of the English language and explores the linguistic and cultural influences that shaped it, including the migration of Germanic tribes to Britain and the impact of Latin and Celtic languages.

Chapter 2: Old English The second chapter focuses on Old English, a period from the 5th to 11th centuries, during which the language was spoken in England. It explores the significant linguistic changes and cultural influences during this time, including the impact of the Vikings and the development of the Anglo-Saxon culture.

Chapter 3: Middle English This chapter covers the Middle English period, from the 11th to the 15th century. It examines the significant linguistic and cultural changes during this period, including the impact of the Norman Conquest and the emergence of Chaucer's Canterbury Tales as a defining work of Middle English literature.

Chapter 4: Early Modern English The fourth chapter delves into Early Modern English, a period from the 15th to the 17th century. It explores the significant linguistic and cultural changes that took place during this time, including the influence of the Renaissance and the development of the printing press.

Chapter 5: Modern English This chapter focuses on Modern English, which began in the late 17th century and continues to this day. It examines the significant historical, social, and cultural contexts that have shaped the language, including the growth of the British Empire, the spread of American cultural influence, and the rise of digital technologies and social media.

Chapter 6: English in the 21st Century The final chapter discusses the role of English as a global language in the 21st century and explores the challenges and opportunities of teaching and learning English. It also reflects on the future of English in a changing world, examining how new digital technologies and emerging cultural and linguistic trends may shape the language in the coming years.

Overall, this book provides a comprehensive and fascinating overview of the English language and its evolution over time, from its ancient origins to its present-day global reach. It is a must-read for anyone interested in the history, culture, and linguistic developments of the English language.

Chapter 1: The Origins of English
The Proto-Indo-European language and its descendants

The English language, like many others around the world, is derived from an ancient language called Proto-Indo-European (PIE). PIE is believed to have originated over 5,000 years ago, somewhere in the region that is now eastern Ukraine or southwestern Russia. It is not a written language, but rather a reconstructed language based on the similarities found among related languages.

The Proto-Indo-European language is the root of a vast family of languages, including most of the languages of Europe, as well as many languages in Asia and parts of the Middle East. The descendants of PIE are divided into several branches, including the Germanic branch, which is the ancestor of English.

The Germanic branch of PIE is believed to have originated in northern Europe, around present-day Denmark and northern Germany. The first Germanic language to emerge from this branch was probably Gothic, spoken by the Goths in the early medieval period. Other early Germanic languages include Old Norse, Old English, and Old High German.

The Germanic branch continued to evolve and diversify over time, resulting in the many Germanic languages we know today, such as German, Dutch, Swedish, and of course, English. English, in particular, has been influenced by a wide range of other languages, including Latin, French, and Norse, as well as the Celtic languages spoken in the British Isles before the arrival of the Germanic tribes.

Despite the vast differences between modern English and its ancient ancestor, the Proto-Indo-European language, linguists have been able to identify a number of similarities between the two. For example, many of the grammatical features of English can be traced back to PIE, including its system of inflection, which is the way in which words change their form to indicate grammatical relationships.

In summary, the English language has its roots in an ancient language called Proto-Indo-European, which also gave rise to a vast family of languages across Europe and Asia. The Germanic branch of this family is the ancestor of English, and it has undergone many changes and influences over time, resulting in the language we know today. Despite its evolution, English still bears some resemblance to its ancient ancestor, a testament to the enduring power of language to connect us to our past.

The Germanic language branch and its relationship to English

The Germanic language branch is one of the most important linguistic branches in the world. It is the root of many modern languages, including English. This chapter will explore the origins of the Germanic languages and their relationship to English.

The Germanic language branch is a subfamily of the larger Indo-European language family. It is believed to have originated in Scandinavia and spread to other parts of Europe through migration and conquest. The Germanic languages are further divided into three main branches: East Germanic, North Germanic, and West Germanic.

English belongs to the West Germanic branch, which also includes German, Dutch, and several other languages. The West Germanic branch can be further subdivided into High German and Low German. English belongs to the Low German group, which is characterized by its use of a number of distinctive features, such as the use of the definite article 'the' and the use of strong and weak verbs.

The Germanic languages are known for their complex inflectional systems, which enable them to express a wide range of grammatical meanings through the use of suffixes, prefixes, and other grammatical markers. However, English has a relatively simple inflectional system, which is believed to be the result of its contact with other languages, such as Old Norse, Old French, and Latin.

English is also notable for its extensive vocabulary, which is believed to be the result of its borrowing from other languages. Many words in English are derived from Latin, French, Greek, and other languages, which have contributed to its rich and diverse vocabulary.

In conclusion, the Germanic language branch has played a crucial role in the development of English, and its relationship to English is an important topic for understanding the language's origins and evolution. The next chapter will delve further into the early history of English, including its Old English period and its transformation into Middle English.

The English language, like all languages, has evolved over time. It has been influenced by various cultures and languages, resulting in a rich tapestry of words and grammar rules that make up modern English.

The earliest known form of the English language is Old English, which was spoken in England from around the 5th century until the Norman Conquest in 1066. Old English was a Germanic language, and its grammar and vocabulary were quite different from modern English.

The earliest known examples of Old English come from a 7th-century manuscript known as the Vercelli Book, which contains a collection of religious poems. These poems are written in a style that is difficult for modern readers to understand, as the language and grammar are vastly different from what we use today.

One of the defining features of Old English is its use of inflectional endings. Nouns, adjectives, and verbs were all inflected to indicate their grammatical function in a sentence. For example, the Old English word "hund" (meaning "dog") would change its form depending on whether it was the subject or object of a sentence.

Old English also had a rich vocabulary, with many words that are no longer used in modern English. For example, "beorg" was an Old English word for "mountain," while "fugol" meant "bird."

Over time, the English language began to change. After the Norman Conquest, French became the language of the ruling class in England, and many French words were incorporated into English. This led to the development of Middle English, which was spoken from the 11th century to the 15th century.

Middle English continued to evolve, and by the time of Shakespeare in the 16th century, the language had changed so much that it is difficult for modern readers to understand without special training.

Despite these changes, many words and grammatical structures from Old English continue to influence modern English. Understanding the earliest forms of the English language can provide insight into the roots of modern English and how it has evolved over time.

The linguistic and cultural context in which Old English emerged

Old English is the earliest known form of the English language, spoken in England from around the 5th century until the Norman Conquest in 1066. The linguistic and cultural context in which Old English emerged was complex and varied, shaped by a number of different factors.

One of the key influences on Old English was the Germanic language family, from which it descended. The Germanic peoples originally migrated from Scandinavia and settled in various parts of Europe, including England. The Old English language was heavily influenced by the Germanic languages of these early settlers, including Norse and Gothic.

In addition to these linguistic influences, the cultural context in which Old English emerged was also significant. During this time period, England was undergoing significant political and social changes. The Anglo-Saxon tribes were warring with each other, and the arrival of the Vikings in the 9th century further destabilized the region. These cultural factors undoubtedly had an impact on the development of the Old English language.

Despite these challenges, Old English flourished as a literary and intellectual language during the Anglo-Saxon period. The language was used to create a rich body of literature, including epic poems like Beowulf and religious works like the Lindisfarne Gospels. Old English was also the language of scholars and intellectuals, who used it to write important works on science, medicine, and philosophy.

As Old English developed and evolved, it underwent a number of changes, including the loss of certain sounds and the adoption of new words from other languages. These changes eventually led to the emergence of Middle English, which was spoken in England from the 11th to the 15th century.

Overall, the linguistic and cultural context in which Old English emerged was complex and varied. However, despite the challenges of this period, Old English managed to thrive as a literary and intellectual language, leaving behind a rich and enduring legacy.

The Anglo-Saxon period and its influence on English

The Anglo-Saxon period, also known as the Early Middle Ages, marked a significant period in the development of the English language. It was a time of great change, upheaval, and conflict, with various Germanic tribes settling in what is now England and interacting with the native Celtic-speaking peoples.

During this time, the Germanic tribes introduced their own languages, which eventually evolved into Old English. Old English was heavily influenced by the Germanic languages spoken by the Anglo-Saxons, such as Old Norse and Old Frisian.

The Anglo-Saxon period was also characterized by a rich oral tradition of storytelling and poetry. This tradition was preserved in the form of epic poems like Beowulf, which provide valuable insights into the language and culture of the time.

Old English is known for its complex grammar and extensive use of inflections, which were used to convey nuances in meaning. Despite its challenges, Old English remained the primary language of England for several centuries.

As England came under the influence of the Norman Conquest in 1066, Old English gradually gave way to Middle English, which was heavily influenced by the Norman French spoken by the ruling class. However, many elements of Old English remain in modern English today, including many of its most basic vocabulary words.

In this chapter, we will explore the Anglo-Saxon period in more detail, examining the linguistic and cultural influences that shaped the development of Old English. We will also delve into the complex grammar and syntax of Old English and examine some of its most famous literary works. By the end of this chapter, readers will have gained a deeper understanding of this critical period in the history of the English language.

The grammar, vocabulary, and pronunciation of Old English

During the Anglo-Saxon period, from the 5th century to the 11th century, the English language underwent significant changes. This period is commonly known as the Old English period, and it saw the development of a distinct English language. Old English is the earliest form of the English language that is comprehensible to modern English speakers, but it is very different from contemporary English.

One of the key characteristics of Old English is its grammar. Old English was a heavily inflected language, meaning that words had different forms based on their role in a sentence. This meant that word order was not as important as it is in modern English. Instead, the endings of words would indicate their grammatical function. For example, the word "sēo" could mean "she," "her," or "it" depending on its context and position in the sentence.

Old English also had a complex system of noun declensions and verb conjugations. Nouns could have up to five cases, depending on their function in the sentence. These cases were nominative, accusative, genitive, dative, and instrumental. Verbs also had multiple forms depending on the tense, mood, and voice of the sentence.

The vocabulary of Old English was heavily influenced by Latin and Greek, as well as the Celtic and Germanic languages. Old English had many words that are still recognizable in modern English, such as "mother," "father," "house," and "fish," but it also had many words that have fallen out of use or have changed in meaning over time.

The pronunciation of Old English was also very different from modern English. It had many more vowel and consonant sounds, and the stress was placed on the first syllable of a word rather than the stressed syllables of modern English.

Overall, Old English was a complex and fascinating language that had a significant impact on the development of English. Despite its differences from modern English, it is still possible to see the roots of our language in Old English.

The Anglo-Saxon period is often regarded as a time of great literary and cultural production in England. During this time, Old English emerged as a fully-formed language, with its own unique grammar, vocabulary, and pronunciation. Old English literature was also produced during this period, including epic poems such as Beowulf, religious texts like the Anglo-Saxon Chronicle, and a wide range of other works.

One of the most notable aspects of Old English literature is its focus on heroic themes and the supernatural. This is perhaps best exemplified by the epic poem Beowulf, which tells the story of a hero who battles a series of monsters and dragons in order to protect his people. Other works of Old English literature, such as the elegiac poem The Wanderer, explore themes of exile, loss, and the transience of life.

In addition to literature, Old English had a significant impact on the development of English culture as a whole. The language was used in religious contexts, with many important religious texts being written in Old English. Additionally, Old English was used in legal and administrative contexts, and many of the words and concepts used in modern English law and government can be traced back to this period.

Old English also had an important influence on the development of the English language more broadly. Many words and phrases from Old English are still in use today, and the grammar and syntax of the language also had a significant impact on the development of Middle English and Modern English.

Overall, the Anglo-Saxon period and the emergence of Old English represent an important turning point in English history and culture. Through their literature, culture, and language, the Anglo-Saxons helped to shape the English-speaking world that we know today.

The historical, social, and cultural contexts of Old English

The Anglo-Saxon period, during which Old English was the dominant language, spanned roughly 600 years, from the fifth century to the eleventh century. During this time, England was home to a number of different Germanic tribes, including the Angles, Saxons, and Jutes, who gradually merged to form a single kingdom.

The language spoken by these tribes was a variant of the West Germanic dialects that had developed from the Proto-Germanic language. This dialect was influenced by the languages spoken by other tribes with whom they came into contact, as well as by Latin, which was the language of the Christian Church.

The social and cultural contexts of Old English were shaped by the pagan beliefs and practices of the Anglo-Saxons, as well as by their conversion to Christianity in the seventh century. Old English literature reflects this cultural shift, with the earliest surviving texts being pagan in nature, while later works are heavily influenced by Christian themes.

The historical context of Old English is characterized by the political instability of the period, with frequent warfare and political upheaval. This instability was reflected in the language, with the emergence of different dialects and regional variations.

Overall, the study of Old English provides a fascinating glimpse into the social, cultural, and historical contexts of early medieval England. Through the analysis of texts and linguistic features, scholars have been able to reconstruct the world of the Anglo-Saxons and gain insight into the development of the English language.

The Norman Conquest and its impact on English

The Norman Conquest of England in 1066 marked a significant turning point in the history of English. Prior to the Conquest, English was the dominant language in England, spoken by the Anglo-Saxon inhabitants of the country. However, following the Norman Conquest, French became the language of the ruling class and the language of law, administration, and literature.

The impact of the Norman Conquest on English was profound. Many French words were introduced into English, particularly in the fields of law, government, and military. This influx of French vocabulary led to a significant expansion of the English language and the emergence of Middle English, the period of English between the 11th and 15th centuries.

Middle English was characterized by a great deal of linguistic diversity, as a result of the mixing of the Old English and French languages. This period saw the emergence of the first English literature, including works such as Chaucer's Canterbury Tales and Sir Gawain and the Green Knight. These works provide valuable insights into the linguistic, social, and cultural contexts of Middle English.

Despite the influence of French on English during the Middle English period, English remained the language of the majority of the population, and the language continued to evolve and develop in new ways. The growth of towns and cities, the expansion of trade and commerce, and the emergence of a middle class all contributed to the development of Middle English and the increasing importance of English as a language of communication and commerce.

Overall, the Norman Conquest had a significant impact on the English language, leading to the emergence of Middle English and the expansion of the English vocabulary. The mixing of French and English during this period helped to create a rich and diverse language that continues to be used and celebrated today.

The development of Middle English grammar and vocabulary

The Norman Conquest in 1066 brought about significant changes to the English language, leading to the development of Middle English. The conquerors, who spoke a dialect of Old French, gradually imposed their language and culture on the English-speaking population, which included Anglo-Saxon, Norse, and Celtic speakers.

Middle English can be considered a transitional period between Old English and Modern English, and it lasted from approximately 1100 to 1500. During this time, English underwent many changes in its grammar and vocabulary, and it became more complex and flexible. One of the most significant changes was the introduction of the definite and indefinite articles, "the" and "a/an," which were not present in Old English.

The vocabulary of Middle English also underwent significant changes. The Norman Conquest introduced many new words of French origin into English, including legal and military terms, such as "court," "jury," and "castle." Additionally, Latin continued to exert its influence on English, especially in the areas of religion and science. Many Latin words were borrowed into Middle English, including "algebra," "crucifix," and "papal."

Middle English also saw the emergence of the first English literature, including the works of Chaucer, who wrote in a dialect of Middle English known as "London English." Chaucer's Canterbury Tales, a collection of stories told by a group of pilgrims on their way to Canterbury, is one of the most famous works of Middle English literature. Other notable works include Sir Gawain and the Green Knight, Pearl, and Piers Plowman.

Overall, the development of Middle English was a significant period in the history of the English language, and it laid the foundation for the development of Modern English. The influence of French and Latin, as well as the emergence of English literature, helped to shape the language into what it is today.

The emergence of English as a literary language during the Middle English period is a fascinating development in the history of the language. Prior to this time, Latin was the dominant language of literature in England, and French was the language of the ruling class. However, the Middle English period saw the rise of a vernacular literature in English, which included works of great importance that are still read and studied today.

One of the most significant literary works of the Middle English period is the epic poem "Beowulf." This poem, which dates to the early 8th century, tells the story of a hero named Beowulf who battles monsters and dragons. It is written in Old English and is considered one of the earliest examples of English literature. While it was not widely known or read during the Middle English period, it would later become an important part of the English literary canon.

Another important work from the Middle English period is "The Canterbury Tales" by Geoffrey Chaucer. This collection of stories, written in Middle English in the late 14th century, follows a group of pilgrims on their journey to the shrine of Saint Thomas Becket. The tales range from bawdy and comedic to serious and moralistic, and showcase Chaucer's mastery of the English language.

Other notable works from the Middle English period include "Sir Gawain and the Green Knight," a medieval romance about a knight's encounter with a supernatural green knight, and "The Pearl," a poem about a father's grief over the loss of his daughter. These works, along with many others, helped establish English as a literary language in its own right, and paved the way for the development of English literature in the centuries that followed.

In addition to literature, the Middle English period also saw the emergence of other forms of written English, including legal and administrative documents, religious texts, and scientific treatises. This growing body of written material helped to standardize the English language and expand its vocabulary, paving the way for the language to become a global powerhouse in the centuries that followed.

Overall, the emergence of English as a literary language during the Middle English period was a significant moment in the history of the language, marking the beginning of a rich tradition of English literature that continues to this day.

Middle English is a period in the history of the English language that spans roughly from the 11th century to the 15th century. During this time, many important historical, social, and cultural events took place, shaping the language and its speakers in numerous ways.

One of the most significant events during the Middle English period was the Norman Conquest of England in 1066. The Normans, who spoke Old French, brought with them their own language and culture, which had a profound influence on English. The ruling class spoke French, and this had a significant impact on the English language. Many French words were introduced into English, which increased the vocabulary of the language and enriched it.

Another significant event was the Black Death, which swept through England in the 14th century. The plague killed a large percentage of the population, which led to social and economic changes. The scarcity of labor and the need to rebuild society had a profound impact on the language, as the remaining population had to adapt and change in response to the new reality.

During the Middle English period, there was also a great deal of literary and cultural activity. English began to emerge as a literary language, and many great works were written during this time, such as Geoffrey Chaucer's "Canterbury Tales." This period saw the development of a new genre of literature, the romance, which would go on to influence literature for centuries to come.

The social and cultural context of Middle English is also important to consider. The period saw significant changes in society, such as the rise of the merchant class, the development of towns and cities, and the emergence of a new middle class. These changes had an impact on the language, as new words were introduced to reflect the new social and economic realities.

In addition, the Middle English period saw the emergence of the English language as a distinct identity. Previously, English had been one of many dialects spoken in the British Isles, but during this period, it began to take on its own identity as a language in its own right. This was due in part to the influx of French words, which gave English a more sophisticated and cosmopolitan character.

Overall, the historical, social, and cultural contexts of Middle English are complex and multifaceted. They reflect the many changes and developments that took place during this important period in the history of the English language, and they continue to influence the language and its speakers today.

Chapter 4: Early Modern English
The Renaissance and the influence of Latin and Greek on English

The Early Modern English period marked a significant time of change and innovation in the English language. During this time, the Renaissance was in full swing, and with it came a renewed interest in classical languages like Latin and Greek. This interest had a profound effect on the English language, and many new words were introduced into the lexicon, as well as new ways of using grammar and syntax.

One of the most significant changes that occurred during this time was the adoption of new words and phrases from Latin and Greek. This was partly due to the increasing availability of classical texts and the influence of humanist scholars who advocated for the study of these languages. As a result, many scientific and philosophical terms entered the English language, such as "algorithm," "anatomy," "biology," and "psychology," to name just a few.

Along with the adoption of new words, the Early Modern English period also saw a shift in grammar and syntax. The use of inflectional endings, which had been a hallmark of Old and Middle English, began to decline, and a greater emphasis was placed on word order and prepositions. This allowed for more complex sentence structures and made it easier to express abstract ideas.

Another significant development during this time was the rise of standardization in English. The publication of the first English dictionary by Samuel Johnson in 1755 helped to standardize spelling and pronunciation, which made it easier for people from different regions to communicate with each other. This was also a time of increased literacy, as more people had access to education, and the printing press made books more widely available.

The Early Modern English period was also marked by significant historical events, such as the English Reformation and the colonization of America. These events had a profound impact on the English language, as religious vocabulary and American English emerged as distinct dialects. The colonization of America also brought English into contact with other languages, particularly Native American languages, which influenced the English lexicon.

In conclusion, the Early Modern English period was a time of significant change and innovation in the English language. The influence of the Renaissance and classical languages, the adoption of new words and syntax, and the rise of standardization and increased literacy all contributed to the development of the English language as we know it today.

In the early modern period, English underwent a significant transformation as it evolved from Middle English to Early Modern English. This period of the English language saw the emergence of many grammatical and linguistic changes, new vocabulary, and a shift in pronunciation.

Grammar:

One of the significant changes in Early Modern English was the simplification of the grammar. The inflectional system of Middle English, which had complex noun and adjective endings, began to disappear, and word order became more rigid. In Early Modern English, nouns became less gendered, and the plural form was standardized with the addition of "-s". Additionally, the use of auxiliary verbs became more widespread, as did the use of the subjunctive mood.

Vocabulary:

The Early Modern English period was a time of great expansion of the English language. This was largely due to the cultural and scientific advancements of the Renaissance, which brought new ideas and concepts to the English-speaking world. Words from Latin and Greek were borrowed and adapted, leading to an increase in the number of polysyllabic words in English. Additionally, the age of exploration brought new words from languages spoken in far-off lands, such as "kangaroo" from the Guugu Yimithirr language of Australia, and "tobacco" from the Taino language of the Caribbean.

Pronunciation:

The pronunciation of Early Modern English was also different from that of Middle English. Vowels became longer, and the distinction between long and short vowels became more prominent. Additionally, the Great Vowel Shift occurred during this period, which caused many long vowels to shift in pronunciation. For example, the word "bite" was pronounced with a long "i" in Middle English, but in Early Modern English, it was pronounced with a diphthong "ai".

The development of Early Modern English had a significant impact on literature and culture. The emergence of printing led to a standardization of the language, making it easier for people to learn and use English. As a result, English became more widely spoken and written, leading to an increase in literature and the arts. Works by Shakespeare and other Renaissance writers helped to establish English as a literary language, and the Bible was translated into English, making it accessible to more people.

Overall, the development of Early Modern English was a crucial period in the history of the English language. The changes that occurred during this period helped to establish English as a language of international importance and set the stage for the further development of the language in the centuries to come.

The role of English in the rise of the British Empire

The Early Modern English period (1500-1700) witnessed a significant expansion of the British Empire, which had a profound impact on the development of the English language. During this period, English became the dominant language of trade, administration, and diplomacy throughout the world. In this chapter, we will explore the role of English in the rise of the British Empire and its impact on the language.

The expansion of the British Empire brought English into contact with many other languages, including Dutch, Portuguese, Spanish, Arabic, Hindi, and Chinese. As a result, English borrowed words and phrases from these languages, enriching its vocabulary and giving it a cosmopolitan character. For example, words like "banana" and "coffee" come from Portuguese, while "candy" and "orange" come from Dutch. The influence of these languages can be seen not only in the vocabulary of English but also in its grammar and pronunciation.

The expansion of the British Empire also led to the spread of English as a second language throughout the world. English became the language of education, science, and technology, and it remains the most widely spoken language in the world today. The spread of English has been facilitated by the growth of international organizations such as the United Nations and the World Trade Organization, which use English as a working language.

During the Early Modern English period, many works of literature were written that reflect the expanding horizons of the British Empire. For example, William Shakespeare wrote plays such as "The Tempest," which explores themes of colonialism and empire. Other writers, such as John Donne and John Milton, wrote poems that celebrate the achievements of the British Empire and its cultural and intellectual superiority.

English became the language of the British Empire not only because of its linguistic qualities but also because of its political and economic power. The British Empire was built on the foundations of trade, and English became the language of commerce and diplomacy. English merchants and traders were able to communicate with their counterparts in other countries, and English became the language of international trade.

In conclusion, the Early Modern English period was a time of great change and transformation for the English language. The expansion of the British Empire brought English into contact with many other languages, and this contact enriched the language and gave it a cosmopolitan character. English became the language of trade, administration, and diplomacy throughout the world, and its spread was facilitated by the growth of international organizations. The literature of the period reflects the expanding horizons of the British Empire and celebrates its cultural and intellectual achievements.

Early Modern English refers to the English language spoken and written in the period between the late 15th and late 17th centuries. This was a time of great change in England, and the language reflected this with a number of new words, phrases, and grammatical structures entering the language.

One of the key historical events of this period was the Protestant Reformation, which had a significant impact on the development of English. The Reformation led to the publication of the first English Bible, which helped to standardize the language and make it more accessible to the general population.

During this time, England also began to establish its dominance as a naval and colonial power, leading to an increased interest in exploration and trade. This resulted in the adoption of words from other languages, particularly those of the countries with which England had commercial ties, such as Arabic, Hindi, and Malay.

Another important historical context was the development of printing technology, which led to an increase in literacy rates and the availability of printed materials, such as books, pamphlets, and newspapers. This helped to spread the English language beyond England's borders and contributed to the standardization of the language.

Socially, the period of Early Modern English was marked by a significant shift in power from the aristocracy to the rising middle class. This led to a greater emphasis on education and literacy, with more people learning to read and write. As a result, the English language became more democratic, with a greater number of people contributing to its development.

Culturally, the Early Modern English period was marked by a flowering of literature, with many of the greatest works of English literature, such as Shakespeare's plays and Milton's Paradise Lost, being written during this time. These works helped to establish English as a major literary language and contributed to the development of its vocabulary, grammar, and syntax.

In addition to literature, the arts and sciences also saw significant developments during this period, with English scientists and philosophers such as Francis Bacon, Isaac Newton, and John Locke making major contributions to their respective fields. These developments helped to establish English as a language of science and scholarship, further cementing its importance in the world.

Overall, the historical, social, and cultural contexts of Early Modern English played a significant role in the development of the language. The Protestant Reformation, England's rise as a colonial power, the development of printing technology, and the growing influence of the middle class all contributed to the growth and standardization of the language. The flowering of literature, science, and the arts during this period also helped to establish English as a major language of culture and scholarship.

Chapter 5: Modern English
The standardization of English grammar and spelling

The standardization of English grammar and spelling is an important aspect of the development of Modern English. Prior to the 18th century, English was not standardized, and there was a great deal of variation in spelling, grammar, and pronunciation across different regions and social classes. The lack of standardization made it difficult for people to communicate effectively and contributed to a lack of prestige for the English language.

One of the most significant developments in the standardization of English was the publication of Samuel Johnson's "A Dictionary of the English Language" in 1755. Johnson's dictionary provided a standard set of definitions and spellings for English words, which helped to establish a common language for all English speakers. Johnson's dictionary also helped to codify many of the grammatical rules of English, which further standardized the language.

Another key development in the standardization of English was the establishment of English as the dominant language of international trade and diplomacy. As the British Empire grew in the 19th and 20th centuries, English became the language of commerce and politics around the world.

This led to a greater demand for standardization, as people from different parts of the world needed to be able to communicate effectively in English.

In the 19th and 20th centuries, efforts were made to standardize English spelling and grammar. One of the most influential figures in this process was Noah Webster, who published "An American Dictionary of the English Language" in 1828. Webster's dictionary helped to establish American English as a distinct dialect of English, with its own spellings and pronunciations. Webster also advocated for simplifying English spelling, arguing that many English words were needlessly complicated.

Despite the efforts of Johnson, Webster, and other language reformers, English remains a highly varied language, with many regional and social dialects. However, the establishment of standard grammar and spelling has made it possible for English speakers around the world to communicate more effectively, and has contributed to the global dominance of the English language.

Today, standard English is the variety of English that is taught in schools and used in formal writing and public speaking. However, there is still a great deal of variation in English, both within and between different English-speaking countries. This variation reflects the rich history and cultural diversity of the English language, and is one of the factors that makes English such a vibrant and fascinating language.

The impact of technology and globalization on English

In the 21st century, the world has become increasingly interconnected, with technology and globalization playing a significant role in shaping the English language. English has become the global lingua franca, and it is estimated that around 1.5 billion people speak English worldwide, with the majority of them being non-native speakers. This globalization of the English language has had a significant impact on its vocabulary, grammar, and pronunciation.

The Influence of Technology

One of the most significant impacts of technology on the English language is the rise of the internet and social media. The internet has provided an unprecedented platform for people from all over the world to communicate with each other, and English has emerged as the primary language of communication. The use of social media has also had a significant impact on the English language. The use of hashtags, emojis, and other forms of shorthand has become increasingly prevalent, particularly among younger generations.

Moreover, technology has also influenced the way people learn and use the English language. Online dictionaries and grammar checkers have made it easier for people to learn and use English, while online courses and language learning apps have become more popular than traditional language schools.

The Influence of Globalization

Globalization has also had a significant impact on the English language. As English has become the language of business and international communication, it has become increasingly important for people from all over the world to learn and use it. This has led to the development of English as a global language, with new words and phrases being added to the language regularly.

Globalization has also led to the emergence of new dialects and accents of English. In countries where English is not the primary language, such as India or Nigeria, English has been adapted to suit the local culture and language. This has led to the development of new dialects, such as Indian English, Nigerian English, and Singaporean English.

English has also been influenced by other languages as a result of globalization. Words from other languages have been adopted into English, particularly from languages such as Spanish, French, and Arabic. This has led to the development of new words and phrases in English, such as "cuisine," "rendezvous," and "safari."

The Impact on Grammar and Pronunciation

The impact of technology and globalization has also affected the grammar and pronunciation of English. The rise of social media has led to the increased use of informal language and colloquial expressions. This has led to a blurring of the line between formal and informal English, with many people using informal expressions in formal settings.

Moreover, the globalization of English has led to the development of new accents and pronunciations of the language. As people from all over the world learn and use English, their native accents and pronunciations have influenced the way they speak the language. This has led to the development of new accents, such as Indian English, and new pronunciations of words.

In conclusion, technology and globalization have had a significant impact on the English language. English has become the global lingua franca, and its vocabulary, grammar, and pronunciation have been influenced by the rise of the internet and social media, as well as the need for people from all over the world to learn and use the language. This has led to the development of new dialects and accents, as well as new words and phrases in English. As technology and globalization continue to shape the world we live in, it is likely that the English language will continue to evolve and adapt to new circumstances.

The evolution of English dialects and accents

The English language has spread throughout the world and has undergone significant changes due to factors such as geography, culture, and social identity. As a result, there are numerous dialects and accents of English spoken around the world today. In this section, we will explore the evolution of English dialects and accents.

Dialects are regional variations of a language that differ in terms of vocabulary, pronunciation, and grammar. These variations arise due to factors such as geography, history, and cultural identity. In the case of English, dialects can be traced back to the early Middle English period, when the language was spoken across England and Scotland.

One of the most well-known dialects of English is Cockney, which originated in the working-class areas of East London. The accent is known for its distinctive pronunciation, which features dropping the 'h' sound at the beginning of words and replacing the 'th' sound with 'f' or 'v'. Cockney also has its own vocabulary, which includes slang words and phrases that are specific to the area.

Another notable dialect of English is American English, which has its roots in the English spoken by early British colonizers who settled in North America. Over time, American English has evolved into a distinct dialect that includes variations in pronunciation, vocabulary, and grammar. For example, American English features the use of words such as "gotten" and "fall" instead of "got" and "autumn," respectively. The accent of American English also differs from that of British English, with differences in the pronunciation of vowels and consonants.

In addition to dialects, English has also evolved into various accents, which are variations in pronunciation that are specific to a particular region or social group. Accents can be influenced by factors such as geography, social class, and ethnicity. For example, the Southern American accent is often associated with the American South and is characterized by the use of a distinct drawl and elongated vowels. The Received Pronunciation accent, on the other hand, is often associated with the upper classes in England and is characterized by the use of non-regional pronunciation.

Technology and globalization have had a significant impact on the evolution of English dialects and accents. The widespread use of social media and other online platforms has led to the creation of new words and phrases, which have become part of the lexicon of various English dialects. Similarly, the ease of travel and migration has led to the spread of English across the globe, resulting in the development of new accents that are influenced by the local languages and cultures of the regions where English is spoken.

In conclusion, the evolution of English dialects and accents is a fascinating reflection of the language's rich history and its spread throughout the world. The variations in vocabulary, pronunciation, and grammar that are present in different dialects and accents reflect the cultural and social diversity of the regions and communities where English is spoken.

The historical, social, and cultural contexts of Modern English

The history of English has been shaped by a variety of factors, including political, economic, social, and cultural changes. In this chapter, we will explore the historical, social, and cultural contexts that have influenced the development of Modern English.

Early Modern English

Early Modern English was the language spoken in England from the late 15th century to the mid-17th century. During this period, English underwent a significant transformation due to several historical and cultural factors. The Renaissance, the Protestant Reformation, and the scientific revolution all contributed to the development of Early Modern English.

The Renaissance was a cultural and intellectual movement that began in Italy in the 14th century and spread throughout Europe in the 16th century. It was characterized by a renewed interest in classical learning, art, and literature. The Renaissance had a profound impact on the English language, as writers and scholars began to draw on the classical languages of Latin and Greek for inspiration.

The Protestant Reformation, which began in the early 16th century, also had a significant impact on Early Modern

English. The reformers rejected the authority of the Roman Catholic Church and advocated for a return to the original teachings of Christianity. As a result, they emphasized the importance of reading and interpreting the Bible in the vernacular languages of Europe, including English.

The scientific revolution, which began in the 16th century, also had a significant impact on Early Modern English. It was a period of great intellectual and scientific advances, and many new words and concepts were introduced into English as a result of the discoveries and inventions of this era.

Standardization of English

During the 18th century, English underwent a process of standardization. The rise of the printing press, the growth of literacy, and the increasing importance of written communication all contributed to the standardization of English. The publication of Samuel Johnson's "A Dictionary of the English Language" in 1755 was a significant milestone in the standardization of English.

Johnson's dictionary was not the first English dictionary, but it was the most comprehensive and influential. It provided a standardized spelling and definition for thousands of English words, and it helped to establish a common standard for written English.

The spread of English

In the 19th and 20th centuries, English became an increasingly global language. The British Empire played a significant role in the spread of English around the world, as the language was used as a means of communication in the colonies. Today, English is the official language of over 50 countries, and it is spoken by over 1.5 billion people worldwide.

The spread of English has been facilitated by technology, particularly the internet. The internet has made it easier than ever before to communicate across borders, and English has become the dominant language of the internet. As a result, the use of English is likely to continue to grow in the coming decades.

Dialects and accents

Despite the standardization of English, there is still a great deal of variation in the way the language is spoken around the world. English has a wide range of dialects and accents, each with its own unique characteristics.

In the United Kingdom, for example, there are a variety of regional accents, including Cockney, Geordie, and Scouse. In the United States, there are also a variety of regional accents, such as the Southern accent and the New York accent.

The dialects and accents of English are influenced by a variety of factors, including geography, social class, and ethnicity. They reflect the diverse cultural and linguistic heritage of English-speaking communities around the world.

*****

As mentioned earlier, English has become a global language and is spoken in many countries worldwide. The English language has evolved and adapted to different contexts, resulting in a wide range of dialects and accents. In England alone, there are numerous regional dialects and accents, such as Scouse, Geordie, Cockney, and Estuary English. Each dialect and accent has unique features in terms of pronunciation, vocabulary, and grammar.

Similarly, in the United States, there are also distinct regional accents, such as the Southern accent, New York accent, and Boston accent. These accents are often associated with particular geographic regions and reflect the history and cultural heritage of those areas. For example, the Southern accent is associated with the American South and is said to have developed from a combination of English, Scottish, and Irish dialects.

Outside of England and the United States, English is also spoken in various countries, such as Australia, Canada, South Africa, and India. Each of these countries has its own unique dialects and accents, influenced by factors such as geography, history, and cultural traditions.

The evolution of English dialects and accents is a fascinating area of study, as it provides insight into the complex social and historical forces that shape language. It also highlights the importance of language as a marker of identity and cultural heritage. As English continues to spread and evolve in different parts of the world, it is likely that we will see new dialects and accents emerging, reflecting the diversity and richness of the English-speaking world.

The role of English as a global language

English has become a global language, with an estimated 1.5 billion people speaking it worldwide. It is the official language of many countries, including the United States, Canada, Australia, New Zealand, and the United Kingdom. English is also the primary language of international business, science, and technology.

The rise of English as a global language can be attributed to various historical, political, and economic factors. During the colonial era, the British Empire spread the use of English across the globe, making it a language of power and privilege. After the Second World War, the United States emerged as a superpower, and the use of English in diplomacy, commerce, and media further solidified its status as a global language.

One of the benefits of English as a global language is that it promotes communication and understanding among people of different cultures and backgrounds. English serves as a common language for international travel, education, and trade. It also facilitates the exchange of ideas and knowledge in fields such as science, technology, and the arts.

However, the dominance of English as a global language has also raised concerns about linguistic and cultural imperialism. Some argue that the spread of English has led to the loss of indigenous languages and cultures. In addition, the standardization of English has created a hierarchy of dialects and accents, with some varieties of English being more valued than others.

Despite these challenges, the role of English as a global language is likely to continue in the 21st century. The rise of digital technologies and the internet has further expanded the reach of English, making it easier than ever to communicate with people around the world. At the same time, the growing awareness of linguistic and cultural diversity is leading to a greater appreciation for the richness and complexity of English in all its forms.

In conclusion, the role of English as a global language has had a profound impact on communication, culture, and society around the world. While it has brought many benefits, it has also raised important questions about power, privilege, and cultural identity. As English continues to evolve and adapt in the 21st century, it will be important to consider these issues and strive for a more inclusive and equitable global community.

The challenges and opportunities of teaching and learning English

English is one of the most widely spoken languages in the world and is considered the language of international communication. As a result, there is a growing demand for English language learning and teaching in various parts of the world. In this section, we will explore the challenges and opportunities of teaching and learning English in the 21st century.

Challenges:

1. Cultural Differences: One of the main challenges in teaching and learning English is cultural differences. English is often taught as a second or foreign language in countries where the language and culture are vastly different from English-speaking countries. This can lead to difficulties in understanding cultural references, idioms, and nuances of the language.

2. Technology: Technology has revolutionized the way we communicate and learn, but it has also presented challenges in the classroom. Students can become easily distracted by technology, and it can be difficult to keep them engaged in the lesson. Additionally, technology can sometimes fail, leading to disruptions in the learning process.

3. Standards and Testing: The standardization of English has led to the development of various tests and exams to assess language proficiency. However, these tests are often based on a narrow definition of language proficiency and can be limiting for students who have a different learning style or cultural background.

Opportunities:

1. Access to Information: With the advent of the internet and social media, students have unprecedented access to information in English. This provides opportunities for students to improve their language skills by engaging with authentic materials such as news articles, videos, and podcasts.

2. Globalization: The increasing interconnectedness of the world has led to a growing demand for English language skills in various fields such as business, science, and technology. This provides opportunities for English language learners to pursue a range of career options and to participate in international exchanges and collaborations.

3. Innovative Teaching Methods: The challenges of teaching and learning English have led to the development of innovative teaching methods such as task-based language teaching, content-based language teaching, and blended

learning. These approaches provide students with more engaging and meaningful language learning experiences.

In conclusion, teaching and learning English in the 21st century present both challenges and opportunities. Educators and learners need to be aware of these challenges and opportunities to effectively navigate the changing landscape of English language education. With a commitment to innovation and a willingness to adapt to new technologies and teaching methods, English language learners can continue to develop their language skills and become successful global communicators.

The future of English in a changing world

The English language has come a long way from its humble beginnings in the Anglo-Saxon kingdoms of early medieval England. Today, it is the most widely spoken language in the world, with an estimated 1.5 billion speakers globally. English has become a global language, used in international communication, business, science, and entertainment. However, the future of English is not without challenges and uncertainties. In this chapter, we will explore the future of English in a changing world.

English as a Global Language

As a global language, English is used in a wide range of contexts, including international trade, diplomacy, science, technology, and the media. The spread of English has been facilitated by several factors, including the influence of British colonialism, the economic and cultural dominance of the United States, and the rise of the internet and social media. English has become a lingua franca, a language of communication between speakers of different languages.

English is used in different varieties around the world, with distinct accents, dialects, and idioms. While British and American English are the most widely recognized varieties, other Englishes, such as Indian English, Nigerian English, and Singaporean English, are also gaining recognition. This diversity of Englishes reflects the global reach and cultural adaptation of the language.

Challenges to English as a Global Language

The global dominance of English has raised concerns about linguistic imperialism, cultural homogenization, and the marginalization of other languages and cultures. Some critics argue that the spread of English has led to the erosion of linguistic diversity and the loss of indigenous languages. They also argue that English has become a tool of power and privilege, favoring those who have access to English education and resources.

The spread of English has also created a demand for English language proficiency, particularly in non-native English-speaking countries. This has led to the commodification of English language teaching and the emergence of a global English language industry, with its own standards, qualifications, and practices. However, this has also led to disparities in English language education and resources, particularly in developing countries and marginalized communities.

Opportunities of English as a Global Language

Despite the challenges, English as a global language also offers opportunities for communication, understanding, and cooperation. English has become a tool for international mobility, social and economic advancement, and cultural exchange. English language proficiency can provide access to global opportunities, such as higher education, employment, and travel. English can also facilitate cross-cultural communication, collaboration, and understanding.

The spread of English has also led to the emergence of new Englishes and hybrid forms of English, reflecting the cultural and linguistic creativity of English-speaking communities. English has become a source of cultural exchange and enrichment, allowing for the exchange of ideas, values, and perspectives.

The Future of English in a Changing World

The future of English is likely to be shaped by several factors, including demographic changes, technological advancements, and geopolitical shifts. The growth of non-native English speakers is likely to increase, particularly in Asia and Africa, leading to the emergence of new varieties of English. The role of English in science and technology is also likely to continue, with English remaining the dominant language of academic research and innovation.

The rise of digital technologies and social media is also likely to shape the future of English. The internet has already facilitated the spread of English and the emergence of new forms of communication, such as texting, social media, and online gaming. These new forms of communication may lead to the emergence of new Englishes, characterized by abbreviations, emojis, and other digital features.

*****

In addition to the impact of technology, demographic changes will also influence the future of English. The world is becoming more interconnected, and people are increasingly mobile, which means that languages are in constant contact and are subject to change. English will continue to be shaped by contact with other languages and cultures, particularly in areas where it is not the dominant language.

Another factor that will shape the future of English is the rise of non-native speakers. Currently, the majority of English speakers are non-native speakers, and this trend is likely to continue. As more people learn English as a second or third language, the language will continue to evolve to meet their needs and preferences.

However, this trend also raises questions about the role of native speakers in shaping the language. Non-native speakers may have different views on what constitutes correct or acceptable English, and they may have different linguistic preferences and practices. This could lead to tensions and debates over what the "correct" form of English should be.

Another challenge for the future of English is the potential loss of linguistic diversity. As English becomes more dominant as a global language, other languages may be threatened and even endangered. This could lead to the loss of valuable cultural and linguistic traditions and knowledge.

To address these challenges, it will be important to promote linguistic diversity and multilingualism. This could involve efforts to preserve and promote minority languages and to ensure that English is learned and used in a way that is sensitive to linguistic and cultural differences.

In conclusion, the future of English is likely to be shaped by a range of factors, including technology, demographic changes, and cultural and linguistic diversity. English will continue to be an important global language, but its role and form may change in response to these trends. It will be important to promote linguistic diversity and multilingualism and to ensure that English is learned and used in a way that is respectful of linguistic and cultural differences.

The historical, social, and cultural contexts of English in the 21st century

The English language has evolved throughout history, influenced by various historical, social, and cultural contexts. In the 21st century, English continues to be a global language, spoken by over 1.5 billion people worldwide. The language is used as a means of communication in a wide range of settings, including business, education, media, and entertainment. In this section, we will explore the historical, social, and cultural contexts of English in the 21st century.

Historical Context

The history of English has been shaped by a variety of historical events, such as the Norman Conquest, the Renaissance, and the British Empire. In the 21st century, English is no longer the language of a single nation, but a global language used in many parts of the world. The rise of English as a global language has been influenced by several historical events, including the growth of the British Empire, the spread of American cultural influence, and the emergence of new technologies.

The British Empire played a significant role in the spread of English around the world. During the 19th and early 20th centuries, Britain established colonies and territories around the world, and English became the language of administration, education, and commerce in these territories. Today, English is still spoken as a first or second language in many former British colonies, such as India, South Africa, and Australia.

Another historical event that influenced the spread of English was the growth of American cultural influence. After World War II, the United States emerged as a dominant economic and cultural power, and American English became the preferred form of English in many parts of the world. Today, American English is the most widely spoken form of English in the world.

Social Context

The social context of English in the 21st century is diverse and complex. English is used by people from different social classes, ethnicities, and cultural backgrounds. The social context of English is influenced by factors such as education, employment, and social status.

English is widely used in education, especially in higher education. Many universities around the world offer courses and programs taught in English. English proficiency is often a requirement for admission to these programs, and students who speak English as a second language may need to take language proficiency tests, such as the TOEFL or IELTS.

English is also used in the workplace, especially in international business settings. Companies that operate in multiple countries often use English as a means of communication between employees from different countries. English proficiency is often a requirement for employment in these companies.

Cultural Context

English is used in a wide range of cultural contexts, such as literature, music, and film. English-language literature is widely read and studied around the world. Many famous authors, such as Shakespeare, Jane Austen, and Ernest Hemingway, wrote in English. English-language literature continues to be an important cultural export of the United Kingdom and the United States.

English is also widely used in music. Many popular songs are written and performed in English, and English-language music is listened to around the world. English-language music has also influenced the development of local music scenes in many countries.

English-language films are also popular around the world. Hollywood films are widely distributed and watched in many countries, and English-language films have influenced the development of local film industries in many parts of the world.

Conclusion

English is a dynamic and evolving language that has been shaped by a variety of historical, social, and cultural contexts. In the 21st century, English continues to be a global language used in a wide range of settings. The historical context of English in the 21st century has been influenced by the growth of the British Empire, the spread of American cultural influence, and the emergence of new technologies. The social context of English is diverse and complex, and English is spoken by people of different ethnicities, social classes, and educational backgrounds. The cultural context of English has been shaped by its use in literature, media, and popular culture, as well as by the diverse linguistic and cultural influences that have shaped its development.

Despite the challenges of teaching and learning English, it remains a highly valuable skill in today's globalized world. The ability to communicate effectively in English opens up opportunities for individuals in a range of fields, from business and finance to science and technology. As the world continues to change and evolve, so too will the role and importance of English.

In conclusion, English has come a long way from its origins as a Germanic language spoken by a few thousand people on the British Isles. It has become a global language used by millions of people around the world, with a rich and complex history that reflects the diversity of its users. As we continue to use and shape English in the 21st century, it is important to understand and appreciate its historical, social, and cultural contexts in order to fully appreciate the richness and complexity of this remarkable language.

Conclusion

A summary of the main points covered in the book

Throughout this book, we have explored the rich and complex history of the English language, from its early origins as a Germanic language to its present-day status as a global language spoken by millions of people around the world. In this concluding chapter, we will summarize the main points covered in the book.

Chapter 1 introduced the concept of language change and discussed the various factors that contribute to language evolution. We examined the history of the English language from its Indo-European roots to its Old English and Middle English forms, tracing the influences of Latin, French, and other languages on English.

Chapter 2 focused on the Early Modern English period, which saw significant changes in English grammar, vocabulary, and pronunciation. We explored the role of Latin and Greek on English during this time, as well as the impact of the printing press and the rise of the middle class on the standardization of English.

Chapter 3 delved into the history of the British Empire and its impact on the spread and development of English worldwide. We discussed the social and political factors that contributed to the growth of English as a global language, as well as the diversity of English dialects and accents that emerged in different parts of the world.

Chapter 4 examined the standardization of English grammar and spelling, tracing the history of prescriptive grammar and the various attempts to codify the rules of English. We also discussed the impact of technology and globalization on English, exploring how the internet and social media are shaping the future of the language.

Chapter 5 focused on the evolution of English dialects and accents, exploring the factors that influence their development and highlighting the diversity of English-speaking communities around the world. We also discussed the historical, social, and cultural contexts of Modern English, examining the ways in which English reflects the values, beliefs, and identities of its speakers.

Chapter 6 explored the role of English as a global language in the 21st century and the challenges and opportunities of teaching and learning English in a rapidly changing world. We also discussed the future of English, examining the ways in which technology, globalization, and cultural diversity are likely to shape the language in the years to come.

In conclusion, this book has provided an overview of the rich and complex history of the English language, tracing its evolution from its Germanic roots to its present-day status as a global language spoken by millions of people around the world. We have explored the various factors that have contributed to the development of English, from the influence of other languages to the impact of technology and globalization. We have also highlighted the diversity of English-speaking communities and the importance of understanding the historical, social, and cultural contexts of the language. Ultimately, this book demonstrates that the study of English is not just about learning grammar and vocabulary, but also about understanding the rich and fascinating history of one of the world's most important languages.

The significance of the English language in human history and culture

English is a language with a rich history and a global presence. It has been shaped by a variety of factors, including geography, politics, culture, and technology, and has in turn shaped human history and culture in significant ways. In this final section, we will explore the significance of the English language in human history and culture, and why it is important to study and understand its past and present.

One of the key reasons why English is significant is its global reach. English is spoken by over 1.5 billion people around the world, making it the most widely spoken language on the planet. It is the language of international business, science, technology, and politics, and is used as a lingua franca by speakers of different native languages to communicate with one another.

English has also played a crucial role in shaping human history and culture. The spread of the British Empire in the 19th and early 20th centuries helped to establish English as a dominant language in many parts of the world. The cultural influence of the United States, which emerged as a global superpower in the aftermath of World War II, further cemented the global importance of English.

English has also contributed significantly to literature, with a rich canon of works spanning from the Middle Ages to the present day. The works of Shakespeare, Milton, Dickens, and other English-language writers have had a profound impact on world literature and culture.

In addition, English has also influenced other languages around the world. The spread of English has led to the emergence of new English-based creole languages, such as Jamaican Patois and Singaporean English. English has also influenced the vocabulary, grammar, and pronunciation of other languages, such as French, Spanish, and Japanese.

Studying the history and evolution of English is important for a number of reasons. First, it helps us to understand the language we use on a daily basis and how it has come to be what it is today. Second, it provides insights into the cultural, social, and political contexts that have shaped the language over time. Finally, it allows us to appreciate the significance of English in human history and culture, and to reflect on its ongoing impact on the world today.

In conclusion, the English language has played a significant role in human history and culture, and continues to be a major global language. Its history is complex and multifaceted, shaped by a range of factors including geography, politics, culture, and technology. Studying the history and evolution of English is important for understanding our world and the language we use to communicate in it.

A reflection on the evolution of English and its ongoing influence in the world today

English has undergone a remarkable evolution over the course of its history, shaped by a variety of factors such as political power, technological advancements, social change, and cultural influence. From its early roots as a Germanic language spoken by a small group of people in the British Isles, English has expanded to become one of the most widely spoken languages in the world, with an estimated 1.5 billion speakers globally.

One of the key factors in the evolution of English has been the influence of the British Empire, which helped spread the language around the world and led to the development of many different dialects and variations of English. As the empire declined and America rose to global prominence, American English began to have a significant impact on the language as well, particularly in the areas of technology, entertainment, and popular culture.

Advancements in technology, particularly the rise of the internet and social media, have also played a major role in the ongoing evolution of English. New forms of communication, such as texting and social media, have given rise to new words and phrases, as well as new conventions for grammar and spelling. The global reach of the internet has also facilitated the spread of English to new populations around the world, leading to the emergence of new Englishes that reflect the cultural and linguistic diversity of their speakers.

Despite its evolution and ongoing diversity, English remains a unifying force in the world today, providing a common language for communication in fields such as science, business, and diplomacy. Its global reach has made it a valuable tool for individuals seeking to connect with people from different cultures and backgrounds, and its influence is likely to continue to grow as the world becomes increasingly interconnected.

English also plays a significant role in shaping cultural and artistic expression, particularly in the areas of literature, music, and film. Many of the greatest works of literature, from Shakespeare to Jane Austen to Toni Morrison, were written in English, and the language continues to be a vehicle for artistic expression and creativity.

At the same time, it is important to recognize that the dominance of English can also create challenges, particularly for those who do not speak the language fluently. As English continues to spread and evolve, it is important to ensure that all individuals have access to the tools and resources necessary to learn and use the language effectively, and to ensure that other languages and cultures are not marginalized or erased in the process.

In conclusion, the evolution of English is a testament to the power of language to shape human history and culture. From its humble beginnings as a regional dialect to its current status as a global language, English has undergone a remarkable journey that reflects the diversity and complexity of the world in which we live. As we look to the future, it is clear that English will continue to play a significant role in shaping our global community, and it is our responsibility to ensure that its ongoing evolution is both inclusive and empowering for all.

To help you better understand the language and concepts related to aging and older adults, below you will find a list of key terms and their definitions.

1. Old English: The earliest form of the English language, spoken in England from around 450 AD to 1100 AD.

2. Middle English: The form of English that was spoken in England from about 1100 AD to 1500 AD, following the Norman Conquest of 1066.

3. Early Modern English: The form of English that was spoken in England from around 1500 AD to 1700 AD, characterized by significant changes in pronunciation, grammar, and vocabulary.

4. Modern English: The form of English that has been spoken in England since around 1700 AD, characterized by continued evolution and standardization of grammar, vocabulary, and spelling.

5. Global English: The form of English that is used as a lingua franca, or common language, around the world, characterized by its use as a second or foreign language by non-native speakers.

6. Dialect: A variation of a language spoken by a specific group of people, often distinguished by differences in pronunciation, grammar, and vocabulary.

7. Accent: The way in which a person pronounces words, influenced by their regional or social background.

8. Standard English: A variety of English that is considered the norm or standard, often used in formal settings and taught in schools.

9. Creole: A language that arises from the mixture of two or more languages, often resulting in a simplified grammar and vocabulary.

10. Pidgin: A simplified form of a language used for communication between speakers of different languages, often lacking a standardized grammar and vocabulary.

Supporting Materials

Introduction:

- Crystal, D. (2003). The Cambridge encyclopedia of the English language. Cambridge University Press.

Chapter 1: The Origins of English

- Baugh, A. C., & Cable, T. (2013). A history of the English language. Routledge.

- Hogg, R. M. (1992). The Cambridge history of the English language. Cambridge University Press.

Chapter 2: Old English

- Mitchell, B., & Robinson, F. C. (2017). A guide to Old English. John Wiley & Sons.

- Lass, R. (1992). Old English: A historical linguistic companion. Cambridge University Press.

Chapter 3: Middle English

- Pyles, T., & Algeo, J. (2010). The origins and development of the English language. Cengage Learning.

- Hogg, R. M., & Denison, D. (Eds.). (2010). A history of the English language. Cambridge University Press.

Chapter 4: Early Modern English

- Fennell, B. A. (2011). A history of English: A sociolinguistic approach. Wiley-Blackwell.

- Nevalainen, T., & Raumolin-Brunberg, H. (Eds.). (2013). Historical sociolinguistics: Language change in Tudor and Stuart England. Routledge.

Chapter 5: Modern English

- McArthur, T. (1998). The English languages. Cambridge University Press.

- Algeo, J. (2006). British or American English?: A handbook of word and grammar patterns. Cambridge University Press.

Chapter 6: English in the 21st Century

- Crystal, D. (2012). English as a global language. Cambridge University Press.

- Graddol, D. (2006). English next: Why global English may mean the end of 'English as a foreign language'. British Council.

Conclusion:

- Crystal, D. (2000). Language death. Cambridge University Press.

- Kachru, B. B. (1985). Standards, codification and sociolinguistic realism: The English language in the outer circle. English in the world: Teaching and learning the language and literatures, 11-30.